To:

_____

From:

_____

Date:

_____

When God Turned On the Light

By Allia Zobel Nolan

Artwork by Linda Clearwater

HARVEST HOUSE PUBLISHERS
EUGENE, OREGON

When God Turned On the Light

Text copyright © 2015 by Allia Zobel Nolan
Artwork copyright © 2015 Linda Clearwater

Published by Harvest House Publishers
Eugene, Oregon 97402
www.harvesthousepublishers.com

ISBN 978-0-7369-4967-5

Design and production by Mary pat Pino, Mary pat Design, Westport, Connecticut

Printed in China.

14 15 16 17 18 19 20 21 22 / DS / 10 9 8 7 6 5 4 3 2 1

I dedicate this book to God, whose love created all that is wondrous, with gratitude for His Son, Jesus—the Light of the world—and His abundant blessings, uppermost of which is my husband, Desmond, whose care, patience, and support light up my world; to my grandfather, Louis Frank; and to my parents, Alvin and Lucille.

Allia Zobel Nolan

It was in the beginning. Things were quiet and dark.
There was no earth or sky. No birds sang. No dogs barked.

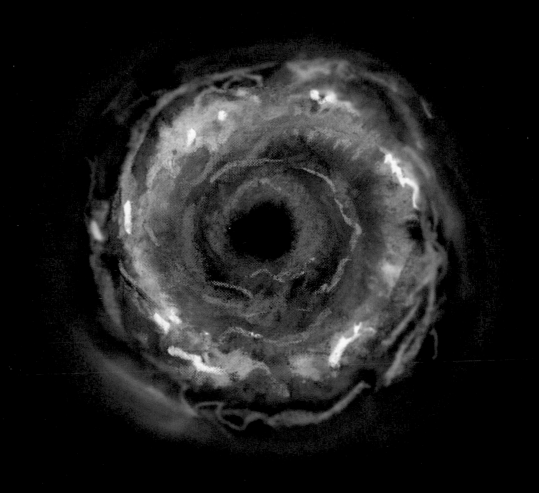

Then God smiled, and a picture of us filled His heart.
Light exploded from love, and the world got its start.

5

When God turned on the light, trees shot up, grass took root.

He made red poppies blossom. Plants bloomed and bore fruit.

Valleys filled with sweet wildflowers that craned their heads, as they drank in the light from their new flower beds.

Rows of mountains appeared—tipped their caps to the light.

Cotton clouds kissed their peaks and then drifted from sight.

Spiders spun sparkly webs.
Inchworms started to crawl.
Soldier ants began marching.
Bees buzzed past them all.

13

Caterpillars munched leaves, which the light made see-through.

When they took off their fuzzy coats, butterflies flew.

Pink flamingos flapped wings.
Toucans squawked with delight.

16

Peacocks preened as their
feathers shone silk in the light.

Lakes lit up like pure diamonds.
Tides danced to and fro.

Scales on fish looked like rainbows.
Eels started to glow.

19

Thirsty zebras drank water and got a surprise—

20

Their reflections were staring them right in the eyes.

Today light still surrounds us. Beams stream from above.

22

God has filled every corner of earth with His love.

23

Light gives life to the stars.
It makes Christmas trees bright.

24

It makes snow look like spun sugar, wispy and white.

Light helps you and me read. It makes Cat think she's tall
As her shadow turns tiger alive on the wall.

Light brings warmth to the day.
It shines out from Mom's smile.
It invites me to stare at the blue sky for a while.

Yes, God lit the world
with another light too.
He was Jesus, the Lord,
who saved me and saved you.

31

Jesus lives in our hearts now. He makes our world bright.
That's what God had in mind when He turned on the light.

You have turned on my light!
The Lord my God has made my
darkness turn to light.

Psalm 18:28